D0726926

ABOUT SCULPTURE

Anthony d'Offay Gallery

9 & 23 Dering Street New Bond Street London W1

01-499 4100

CARL ANDRE

Aluminium-Copper Alloy Square
Düsseldorf 1969
Aluminium and copper
100-unit square
50 plates of each metal
Overall size $5/16$ x $78\frac{3}{4}$ x $78\frac{3}{4}$ in

JOSEPH BEUYS

Tisch mit Aggregat
1958/85
Bronze
Height 39 in
Signed and numbered 2/4

GILBERT AND GEORGE

Bloody Life No 14
Sculpture Spring 1975
Photo-piece
97 x 81 in
Signed and dated

BLOODY LIFE

WILLEM DE KOONING

Small Seated Figure

1973
Bronze
Height   20¾ in
Signed and numbered 7/7

JANNIS KOUNELLIS

Untitled
1987
Steel, lead and beeswax
78¾ x 71 in

RICHARD LONG

Marble Fields
1986
White marble
56 x 14 ft

MARIO MERZ

Igloo, 'Hoarded centuries to pull up a mass
of algae and pearls' (Ezra Pound)
1983
Metal, glass, sulphur and neon
Height 85½ in   diameter 157½ in

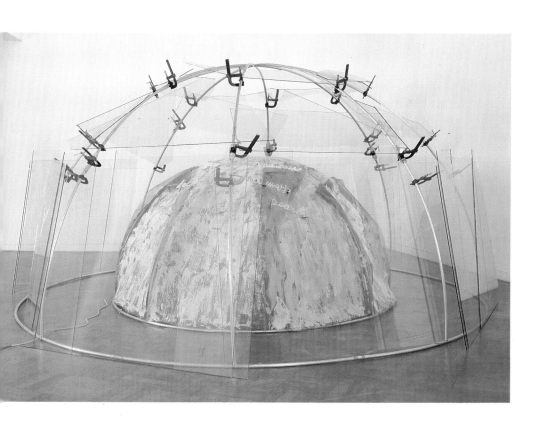

BRUCE NAUMAN

Marching Man
1985
Neon tubing
70¾ x 52½ in
Unique

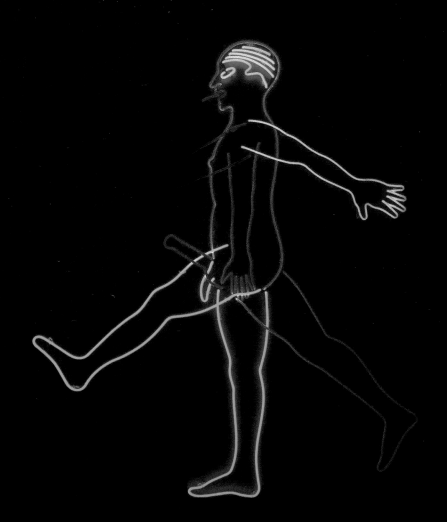

DAVID SMITH

Circles Intercepted
1961
Steel, painted white, green, red,
yellow, brown, blue, violet and black
89½ x 56 x 20 in
Signed and dated 3-2-1961

CY TWOMBLY

Untitled

1959
Painted resin
21½ x 14⅛ x 10¼ in
Signed and numbered 3/6

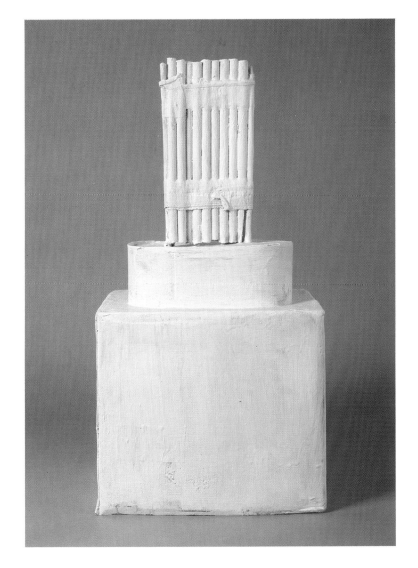

BOYD WEBB

Lung
1983
Unique colour photograph
45¼ x 59¾ in

LAWRENCE WEINER

BILLOWING CLOUDS OF FERROUS OXIDE
SETTING APART A CORNER ON THE BOTTOM
OF THE SEA
1986

BILLOWING CLOUDS OF FERROUS OXIDE SETTING APART A CORNER ON THE BOTTOM OF THE SEA

ISBN 0 947564 11 X

© 1988 Anthony d'Offay Gallery
Photography by Prudence Cuming Associates
and Dorothy Zeidman (Bruce Nauman)
Designed by Simon Rendall
Colour separations by System Colour
Printed by Four Print